AS Government & Politics

UNIT 1

Edexcel

Unit 1: People & Politics

Chris Robinson

Philip Allan Updates
Market Place
Deddington
Oxfordshire
OX15 0SE

Orders
Bookpoint Ltd, 130 Milton Park, Abingdon, Oxfordshire, OX14 4SB
tel: 01235 827720
fax: 01235 400454
e-mail: uk.orders@bookpoint.co.uk
Lines are open 9.00 a.m.–5.00 p.m., Monday to Saturday, with a 24-hour message answering service. You can also order through the Philip Allan Updates website: www.philipallan.co.uk

© Philip Allan Updates 2005

ISBN-13: 978-1-84489-007-1
ISBN-10: 1-84489-007-4

This guide has been written specifically to support students preparing for the Edexcel AS Government & Politics Unit 1 examination. The content has been neither approved nor endorsed by Edexcel and remains the sole responsibility of the author.

Printed by MPG Books, Bodmin

Environmental information
The paper on which this title is printed is sourced from managed, sustainable forests.

P00843

Contents

Introduction

The aim of this guide is to prepare students for the Unit 1 People & Politics examination for the Edexcel Advanced Subsidiary (AS) GCE in Government & Politics. Unit 1 introduces the study of politics by looking at the central ideas of citizenship, democracy and participation, and by examining the representative processes in the UK. It is important that you gain a secure understanding of these topics because the other AS units develop many of them further. The specification for People and Politics can be divided into four main topics:

(1) Political participation and democracy: key concepts such as power and authority, legitimacy and democracy, rights and freedoms.

(2) Elections: the relationship between elections and democracy; the different types of electoral system; referendums.

(3) Political parties: the functions of political parties; their traditions; their relationship with the democratic process.

(4) Pressure groups: different categories of pressure group; their activities; the factors that contribute to their success; the extent to which these groups enhance the democratic process.

How to use this guide

This **Introduction** contains information about the format of the unit test and how your answers will be marked, as well as advice on revision and how to approach the various types of question on the examination paper.

The **Content Guidance** section summarises the knowledge and skills that are needed to succeed in the Unit 1 examination. It provides an overview of each topic and focuses on the themes that most commonly arise in the examination.

The **Question and Answer** section contains a range of questions which might be found on the People & Politics exam paper. The answers and examiner comments concentrate on the essentials needed to gain high marks.

Scheme of assessment

The AS GCE has a weighting of 50% when carried forward towards the full A-level GCE. The structure of the AS course is as follows:

Unit	Assessment method	Length	Objectives assessed
1	Written — 2 structured questions from a choice of 4	1 hour	1 (50%), 2 (30%), 3 (20%)
2	Written — 2 structured questions from a choice of 4	1 hour	1 (50%), 2 (30%), 3 (20%)
3	Written — 1 stimulus question from a choice of 2, both consisting of 3 or 4 stepped parts	1 hour	1 (50%), 2 (30%), 3 (20%)

There are three assessment objectives (AOs), or sets of skills, that you will be tested on in the examination. In Unit 1, AO1 has a higher weighting than AO2 and AO3. The skills required by each AO are shown in the table below.

Assessment objective	Skills required	Unit 1 weighting
AO1	recall, select and deploy knowledge of government and politics accurately, showing understanding of relevant political concepts and theories	50%
AO2	analyse and evaluate political information, arguments and explanations, and identify parallels, connections, similarities and differences between the aspects of the political systems studied	30%
AO3	communicate arguments and explanations in a clear and structured manner, making use of a range of relevant evidence and appropriate political vocabulary	20%

Exam format

Unit 1 is assessed in a 1-hour exam. In this time you have to answer two questions from a choice of four, which means you have 30 minutes to answer each question.

Each question is subdivided into three parts. If you divide the 30 minutes up in proportion to the marks available for each part of the question, this gives you an indication of how long you should spend on each part:

- **Part (a): 5 marks (3 minutes approximately)**
  These questions usually require you to write a short definition, description or distinction. As you only have 3 minutes in which to do this, your answer must be concise. A couple of relevant points briefly explained, with an example if appropriate, is all that is needed to get full marks. One useful practice technique is to find out exactly how much you can write in 3 minutes. This can then act as a rough guide as to how long your answer should be.
- **Part (b): 15 marks (9 minutes approximately)**
  Clearly, more substance is expected in answers to part (b) questions than part (a) ones. You should aim to make a number of points (sometimes the number is specified in the question), which should be supported by explanations and evidence in the form of appropriate examples, quotes or data.
- **Part (c): 30 marks (18 minutes approximately)**
  Responses to part (c) questions should be substantial — about twice as long as your part (b) responses. You are expected to offer a range of points that are fully supported by evidence and explanation. When evaluation is required (e.g. if a question begins 'To what extent'... or 'What are the advantages and disadvantages of...'), you must give both sides of the argument in order to achieve high marks.

Revision advice

There are two basic reasons why candidates underperform in this examination:
(1) inadequate preparation
(2) failure to answer the question set

Some students adopt a very systematic approach to exam preparation: they ensure that they understand fully the principles of electoral systems, for example, before moving on to revise the next topic. At the other extreme, there are those who believe that revision makes no difference. In the middle, there are those students who indulge in 'comfort revision'. This involves simply going over and over the notes and essays of topics with which they are familiar, and putting aside topics which have proved to be more problematic. Comfort revision is at best a waste of time and at worst will probably lead to serious underperformance in the exam.

A key strategy for using your revision time more effectively is to categorise your notes as follows:

- **Category 1:** notes and essays on topics with which you feel confident and which you understand well.
- **Category 2:** notes and essays on topics with which you feel reasonably happy, but think may need attention before you can answer a part (c) question on the topic.
- **Category 3:** notes and essays on topics which you do not understand and which you would prefer to forget.

When revising, you should allocate time to your Category 2 and 3 topics. You are likely to see a greater return on a given amount of revision on a topic with which you have struggled in the past than on one with which you are already conversant. The idea is to raise all topics up to or close to the level of your Category 1 topics. For this to have any chance of working, you must be honest about which topics are a problem and either consult this guide and other books or discuss the difficulty with your teacher.

You should revise all the topics on the Unit 1 specification. Failing to revise any one of them could leave you with limited choices in the exam.

Examination skills

Read the questions

Before you start, take time to read the question paper properly. When reading a question, look for the key words on which your answer will hinge. Consider this example:

(c) Make a case for the wider use of referendums. (30 marks)

This question is asking you to make points on *one* side of the debate about whether referendums are a good thing or not. If you give arguments against the wider use of referendums as well as in favour of them, or write everything there is to know about referendums, you will not gain any extra marks and you will have wasted valuable time. This might appear obvious, but you would be surprised how many candidates missed the key words when this question was set. Practise finding the key words in questions on old exam papers. Words such as 'coherent', 'change', 'impact' and 'extent' radically affect the manner in which you should approach a question.

Plan your answers

Some candidates write plans for all their answers at the beginning of the exam. Although this takes time, it can be beneficial. If you plan your answer to all parts of a question before you start writing, you can be sure that you will have enough information to answer part (c) effectively. It is far better to spend a few minutes doing this than to get to part (c) of a question and realise that you do not know enough to answer it.

Plans help you to order and reorder your ideas prior to committing them to paper. They enable you to build up your essay in a logical way that is more likely to impress an examiner than randomly stated points. Plans can also come in useful if you run out of time — if your plan remains without crossings out, the examiner will consider the points made in it and give you some credit for them, especially if you annotate them.

Follow the rubric

The unit test requires you to answer two out of the four questions. Each question is divided into three parts. **You must answer the correct number of questions**. If you fail to answer one, your overall mark will be seriously reduced as a result. Similarly, if you answer more than two questions, your overall mark will be reduced because there is not enough time to answer more than two questions properly.

You should be familiar with the format of the exam. Copies of past papers can be obtained from Edexcel and the subject specification is available on the Edexcel website (**http://www.edexcel.org.uk**).

Manage your time

Organising your time in the examination itself is just as crucial as good preparation beforehand. All examination rooms must have clearly visible clocks and you should jot down somewhere, either on your question paper or answer book, the times by which you should be beginning each new question. You should then stick to this timetable.

Although it is tempting to devote disproportionate time to questions you know you can answer well, it is not advisable to spend too long on the 5-mark questions — no matter how much you write in answer to these, the maximum you can achieve is 5 marks. This may seem obvious, but many examiners comment on how some scripts have longer responses to the 5-mark questions than to the 15- or 30-mark questions.

The best way to manage time is to practise. Use the Question and Answer section at the end of this book to practise your examination technique against the clock.

Practical tips

- **Do questions have to be answered in any particular order?** No. Some candidates offer what they consider to be their strongest answer first. This approach can help to focus your mind and boost your confidence.
- **Some candidates deliberately leave their responses to the very short answer questions until the end of the paper — is this advisable?** There is some logic to this practice, particularly if you are worried about your time management. However, badly answered questions, whether short or long, will lose you marks.
- **What should you do if there are only 10 minutes left and you still have a part (c) to answer?** If you only have 10 minutes left, the best thing to do is to convert a plan into a series of briefly explained bullet points. Although this will not earn

as many marks as a full answer, it is likely to earn more than a partial response to the question that ends with the words 'Sorry, ran out of time'. It is important to remember that time management is a skill which is implicitly being assessed in the examination and that weakness in this respect will cost you marks.

- **What should you do if you are not short of time but feel there are no more questions that you can answer?** One thing is certain in examinations: if you do not attempt a question, you will earn no marks for it. It is better to answer a question badly than not to attempt it at all. Even if you only earn 10 marks out of 30 for a part (c) answer, this could mean the difference between a grade E and a grade C.

Content Guidance

This section outlines the key content of the AS specification for Unit 1. It is broken down into the four main topics assessed in the Unit 1 test:

(1) Democracy and participation

This topic examines the key concepts that underpin the institutions and processes that are covered in the other three topics (and indeed in the other AS units in the specification).

(2) Elections

This topic includes the main electoral principles, the different types of electoral system and the impact that they have in the areas in which they are used in the UK. There is also an examination of the role of referendums in the UK.

(3) Political parties

The functions of political parties, the ideas that underpin them, and an assessment of the current Conservative and Labour positions with regard to key policy areas are considered in this topic.

(4) Pressure groups

This topic examines the main types of pressure groups and evaluates their activities and the role they play in the UK system of democracy.

Democracy and participation

Power and authority

These are important concepts in the study of politics. Two hundred years ago, power had little to do with the will of the people in the modern sense. Similarly, ordinary citizens were not expected to participate in the governing of the country. Today, however, the role of citizens in the exercise of power and authority is crucial for the effective working of politics.

Power

Power relates to the ability to get someone or a group of people to do what you want them to do — even if it is against their will. There are various manifestations of power. Military power, for example, uses force to get others to comply. Economic power is also important nowadays, as evidenced by the acceleration of the globalised economy over the past 20 years.

Political power can result from either military or economic power. A glance into history indicates just how important military might was for keeping rulers in power. Similarly, the economic clout of countries such as the USA gives them considerable leverage over smaller countries that are keen to benefit from aid and other support packages.

Authority

Authority implies the right to tell people what to do or a right to govern. There are three main types of authority:

(1) Traditional authority. This is when rulers call for the consent of the people. This has appealed for centuries on the basis of continuity, history, respect for royal and political institutions and religious tradition.

(2) Authority based on the charisma of the leader. Many regimes build up a so-called 'cult of personality' in order to maintain the compliance of their people. Stalin, Hitler and Mao Zedong are all examples of leaders using charisma to devastating effect. These are extreme examples, but even in the UK variations in the amount of charisma displayed by political leaders can affect their authority. Compare Margaret Thatcher, John Major and Tony Blair.

(3) Legal, rational authority. This forms the cornerstone of all Western liberal democracies. The right of the government to govern is based on the fact that it was elected into power and has the legitimate authority of the people to rule the country.

Authority in the UK is based on all three of the above. At times, certain types of authority may prevail more than others. It could be argued, for example, that when John Major was prime minister, charismatic authority was not in abundance. A useful exercise is to write all three types of authority on a piece of paper and beside each one describe how they are manifested in the UK political system at the present time; then compare this with the situation when other governments were in power.

Types of democracy

Democracy is when the people are able to exercise their will in political matters. It can be direct, e.g. when voters express views that will determine specific policy outcomes, or indirect, e.g. when representatives are elected to decide on the voters' behalf.

Direct democracy

Democracy literally means people power and direct democracy is when all the people in a state make all the decisions affecting them on a daily basis. In ancient Athens all qualified citizens were able to decide the major issues that affected them. In the modern state, however, direct democracy would be unworkable, given the millions of people there are and the myriad of issues on which to decide. Society would probably cease to function if attempts were made to run it as a direct democracy.

Representative democracy

The concept of representative democracy is based on the idea that in a large and complex society it is not possible to involve everyone in the decision-making process. Electing representatives to take decisions on behalf of its citizens enables such a society to achieve democratic characteristics. Representatives may be local councillors in the town halls or MPs in the House of Commons. As such, representative democracy can be regarded as indirect democracy, as distinct from direct democracy.

Features of representative democracy

One of the most important features of a representative democracy is an **election**. This enables chosen representatives to govern on behalf of the people and should ensure that government and parliament reflect and respect the opinions of the people. In this sense, the political direction that a country takes should be in tune with the national mood. When Labour came to power in 1997 it was following an election in which the people demonstrated their desire for a change in political direction. Elections convey legitimacy in that they provide the basis for a government's authority.

Another feature of representative democracy is that the government (the House of Commons in the UK) should **reflect the society it seeks to represent**, both in terms of political opinion, represented in the views of the various political parties in parliament, and in terms of the social, ethnic and gender groups in society. In other words, elected representatives should bear a resemblance to the people who elect them to office. In order to get more women into the House of Commons, the Labour Party has had a policy of all-women short lists for candidates in many of its safest seats. Previously the '300 Group' of women MPs campaigned for better female representation in the Commons. All the major political parties are also striving for more parliamentary candidates from the ethnic minorities.

Accountability is another important feature of representation. In the UK, representatives must periodically be answerable for the decisions that they make. If they want to be re-elected, their actions need to come under public scrutiny. Elections enable the process of accountability in a representative democracy.

A final aspect of representation may be described in a negative sense. In the UK, representatives are **not mere delegates**. MPs are elected to govern as well as to represent. On occasions, this may involve public opinion being overlooked, even if this proves to be unpopular. If political expedient is outweighed by the judgement of the representative, then decisions may be taken which might anger the public. Many MPs used this argument to justify their decision to support the invasion of Iraq in 2003. Ultimately, the people have the final say at general elections following contentious decisions.

Democracy in the UK

The table below summarises the points that can be brought into an answer on whether or not the UK is a democracy. Use them as a starting point for further reading or for revision purposes.

Elements of democracy in the UK	Limitations to democracy in the UK
• Free and fair elections held at regular intervals	• Elections are not free financially and the government gets to choose the time of the election
• Political parties are free to air their views and campaign for their policies	• Smaller political parties may suffer as a result of the electoral system
• Politicians are accountable to the people at election time	• Accountability is blurred; most people vote for or against the party, regardless of the calibre of the sitting MP
• Freedom of speech	• Limitations on speech regarding race; laws on defamation
• Free press	• Limits on issues to do with national security; libel laws
• Freedom of association	• Some restrictions on the activity of trade unions
• Freedom of assembly	• The police may break up assemblies that they deem riotous
• No official discrimination against minority groups	• Discrimination still persists in key areas such as employment and housing
• Human Rights Act	• Human Rights Act is just an act — rights are not as enshrined as they are in the USA, for example

There is much debate about the nature of UK democracy. Despite the limitations outlined above, the UK is a democracy when compared to some countries in the world where democracy is more suspect, for example where:

- elections are rigged
- leaders are corrupt
- human rights are violated
- people have no say in how they are governed

However, some countries appear to be more democratic than the UK in certain respects because they:
- protect the rights of their citizens in a more secure way
- place firmer limits on the actions of governments
- have fairer voting systems

Recent developments in UK democracy

Some people claim that the UK has become a more democratic country since the election of the Blair government in 1997. During this time, the government has introduced a number of constitutional reforms, which have in the eyes of many on the centre left transformed a constitution of the nineteenth century into something approaching one for the twenty-first century. Conservatives would argue that these reforms have done nothing to make the UK more democratic. Indeed, they would claim that the massive parliamentary majorities wielded by Labour since 1997 have turned the UK into an elective dictatorship. Others, such as the Liberal Democrats, argue that New Labour has failed to tackle the key inadequacies of the UK's democratic system and has merely tinkered with the margins.

Devolution

Labour has decentralised power in the UK. After the 1997 general election, Labour fulfilled its promise of offering devolution to Scotland and Wales. This development can be seen as bringing politics closer to the regions of the UK. The reasoning behind this is that the best people to govern major aspects of Scottish public policy are the Scots themselves. These reforms mark a break with the tradition that political power is in the hands of the government in Westminster.

Referendums

Labour held referendums in Scotland and Wales on the issue of devolved assemblies. Until November 2004, when voters in a referendum in the North East turned down a proposal to establish an elected regional assembly, the government was keen to push ahead with referendums for such assemblies in England. The Blair government has sharply increased the use of referendums, and has promised to consult the country over the issues of the EU constitution and the European single currency. This use of referendums can be seen as a move to more direct democracy in the UK.

Proportional representation

The new devolved assemblies are elected using systems of proportional representation and it can be argued that the basis for representation in the Scottish Parliament and National Assembly for Wales is more democratic than that for the House of Commons, which continues to use the first-past-the-post system. In addition, since 1999 proportional representation has been introduced for elections to the European

Parliament. As a result, MEPs representing smaller political parties, such as the Green Party and the UK Independence Party (UKIP), have been elected; at the European elections in 2004, UKIP won over ten MEPs.

Reform of the House of Lords

One of the long-standing constitutional headaches for the Labour Party has been the House of Lords. After failing to reform the second chamber in the late 1940s and late 1960s, when Labour was previously in power, the Blair government has taken the significant step of abolishing most of the hereditary peers in the House of Lords. This is the first stage of a two-part process of reform. Supporters of the move believe that the hereditary peers were a symbol of undemocratic politics in the UK.

Human Rights Act (1998)

The government has introduced the Human Rights Act, which for the first time sets out clearly the rights that citizens enjoy. Previously, citizens' rights were based on being able to do anything that the law had not yet proscribed, i.e. so-called negative rights. Citizens no longer need to seek redress from the European Court of Human Rights in Strasbourg if they feel that their rights have been curtailed. The Human Rights Act has effectively incorporated the European Convention of Human Rights into English and Scottish law.

Criticisms of UK democracy

Some people argue that the UK has not become more democratic in recent times.

Electoral reform for the House of Commons

The government has changed its mind about a promise the Labour Party made before the 1997 general election, which was to hold a referendum on electoral reform for the House of Commons. Despite other bodies having new systems, arguably the key decision-making body in the UK remains controlled by a political party with fewer than half of the votes cast in the country. Supporters of electoral reform in parties such as the Liberal Democrats and in groups such as the Electoral Reform Society accuse the government of having only a half-hearted commitment to the issue. They argue that when it comes to reforms affecting where the real power is, the government has failed to act in order to preserve more power for itself.

Reform of the House of Lords

The government can be criticised for not completing the reform of the Lords and Tony Blair in particular appears to want to resist having an elected second chamber. Given the fact that an appointed chamber always gives rise to the suspicion that its composition is controlled by the government, Blair will remain under some pressure from reformers on this issue.

Human Rights Act

The Human Rights Act is not an entrenched document. It is another Act of Parliament which can be amended or even repealed at some future date. Critics argue that this has already started, as it was amended almost as soon as it became law in order to restrict the rights of terrorist suspects. Many civil rights groups have called for a written constitution containing a bill of rights — they argue this is the only way to protect the rights of the citizen fully.

Elections

The electoral mandate

An electoral mandate is a right to govern. It is the basis upon which all the decisions made by our political leaders are legitimised: governments can carry out their legislative programme if they have the consent of voters to do so. The mandate is often confused with a party manifesto, but although there is clearly a link between the two, they are not the same. The electoral mandate implies that governments should stick to their manifesto commitments once they have been elected to govern.

There are varying interpretations of the electoral mandate. It can be argued that, regardless of the electoral system in use, the government does not necessarily enjoy the support of a majority of voters. This means that defenders of the first-past-the-post electoral system see no conflict between an electoral system that regularly delivers government parliamentary majorities without majorities of the vote and the notion of a popular mandate.

Critics of the UK system for electing MPs do not agree with this point of view. They argue that an electoral mandate should convey the wishes of the majority of the electorate, and any government ought to feel that it has this level of support before committing to policy options.

Electoral principles

The main principles that underpin the organisation and conduct of elections in the UK are summarised in the following table.

Elections should be free and fair	Elections should be transparent
• Universal suffrage	• They should be easy to understand
• Regular elections	• Voting papers should be laid out clearly
• Secret ballot	• Counting should be accessible to all candidates
• No intimidation of voters	• The result should be administered fairly
• Conducted honestly	• The result should be accepted as accurate

Elections should be politically free	Elections should be seen to be legal
• Freedom of speech	• Results can be challenged in a recount
• Parties free to organise campaigns	• Results can be challenged in court
• Free assembly	• Ballot papers can be traced
• Press has free political coverage	• Judges should be able to declare elections void
• No state propaganda	• Candidates who cheat should not profit from their actions

Electoral systems

There are a variety of electoral systems in use in different parts of the UK. This section examines plurality, majoritarian and proportional systems.

Plurality systems

Simple plurality

This is more commonly known as the first-past-the-post system. It is used for parliamentary and local council elections in the UK, and for presidential and congressional elections in the USA.

The candidate with a plurality of votes, i.e. at least one more vote than the candidate coming second, wins the seat. The system is a 'show of hands' type of arrangement. Until the 1870s, that is exactly how elections were conducted in the UK — the winner was declared after counting the number of arms raised in support of the candidates at public gatherings.

In the UK, this system operates at both constituency level, when the individual MP is elected, and national level, when seats are taken in the House of Commons. The party with the majority of seats in the Commons (after the results of the elections in each of the constituencies have been declared) becomes the government.

Effects of the simple plurality system

A candidate can win a constituency seat even if he or she receives less than 50% of the votes cast. The more candidates there are standing for a particular seat, the lower the percentage of votes required to win: technically, if ten candidates stand, one of them could win with a little over 11% or 12% of the vote.

At national level, when all these votes and seats are aggregated, the winning party (i.e. the one with the majority of seats which will become the government) often does not have a majority of votes. For example, in the UK general elections of 1997 and 2001, Labour was elected to power with about 44% and 41% of the vote respectively. No party has achieved a majority of the votes in a general election since the Second World War.

Majoritarian systems

Majoritarian systems are designed to ensure that the winning candidate in a particular contest has the support of at least 50% of those people who voted in the election.

Supplementary vote

This system has been used for electing the London mayor since 2000. It follows the same principle as the alternative vote, which is used for elections to the House of Representatives in Australia. Voters rank their two favoured candidates on the ballot paper in order of preference: '1' for their first choice, '2' for their second choice. (In the alternative vote system, voters can place preferences against *all* the candidates on the ballot paper.)

For a candidate to win, he or she has to achieve over 50% of the first preference votes. If no candidate achieves this, the candidate with the fewest first preference votes is eliminated from the counting and all of his or her second preference votes are reallocated to the remaining candidates. This process continues until one candidate has over 50% of the vote.

In the 2004 elections for the London mayor, no candidate achieved more than 50% of the first preference votes. Ken Livingstone for the Labour Party was in first place and Steve Norris for the Conservatives was in second place. After the reallocations from eliminated candidates, Ken Livingstone crossed the 50% barrier and was elected mayor for the second time.

Effects of the supplementary vote system

This system ensures that the candidate who is elected has the support of over 50% of those who turned out to vote. However, it does encourage parties to come to deals beforehand, urging voters to 'Vote Smith 1, vote Jones 2', for example. As such, it may promote more collaborative politics.

If this system were used to elect an entire assembly, there is no guarantee that the governing party would have over 50% of the votes. The problem is that not all seats are the same size and turnouts vary between constituencies, as does the size of the winning candidate's majority. Add up these factors across 659 individual results and anomalies begin to emerge; the chance of a government gaining a parliamentary majority without a majority of the national vote becomes distinctly possible, especially if the parliamentary majority is a narrow one.

The system therefore remains as flawed, at least as far as the national result is concerned, as the simple plurality (first-past-the-post) system. Many adherents of electoral reform reject this system because it lacks proportionality and is unfair to some political parties.

Proportional systems

Proportional representation is a general term that refers to any electoral system designed to achieve an election result in which the number of seats that a party receives is in proportion to the percentage of votes that the party wins. There are a number of proportional systems and, depending on which system is used, there can be a variation in the degree of proportionality achieved. Factors that may vary from system to system include the number of representatives elected in each constituency, the presence of preferential voting, and whether voters choose from a list of candidates or simply choose a party. The systems outlined below are used for at least one type of election in the UK.

Regional party list

This system is used for UK elections to the European Parliament. The UK is divided into 12 large multi-member constituencies, which return more than one representative to the Parliament. There are 78 MEPs altogether. Voters vote for a party and the parties publish lists of candidates. The bigger the percentage of votes that a party receives, the greater the number of names elected from its list. The UK system comprises closed lists, so-called because the voters have no way of choosing between candidates from any list.

The system is also closed in the sense that it is the party that determines the names of candidates who appear on its lists and the order in which they appear (the closer a candidate is to the top of the list, the greater his or her chances of getting a seat).

Effects of the regional party list system

This system has made some big differences to party representation in the UK. The simple plurality (first-past-the-post) system tended to favour Labour and the Conservatives, because of the solidity of their support in their respective strongholds. Using the list-based system described above resulted in parties such as the Greens and the UK Independence Party gaining national representation for the first time ever in 1999. In 2004 UKIP managed to win 12 seats in the elections to the European Parliament — this would not have been possible without using a proportional electoral system.

The closed nature of the list system as it operates in the UK has been a source of some concern because it gives the leadership of the political parties the power to determine where an individual name appears on the list. This system has also ended the direct link between the constituent and the MEP (in London, for example, 9 MEPs are returned).

There is an open list variant of this system in which voters not only get to choose their party, but also tick the name of their preferred candidate. Many argue that this is a fairer system that empowers the elector and reduces the influence of the party leadership.

Single transferable vote (STV)

This system is used to return members to the Northern Ireland Assembly. It uses multi-member constituencies and, like the supplementary vote system, preferential voting (although the voter can express more than just a first and second choice).

The aim of the system is to achieve a proportional result and not just a majority for the winning candidate. To achieve this outcome, candidates must reach a quota in order to be elected. This is calculated by the following formula:

$$\frac{\text{votes cast}}{\text{seats} + 1} + 1$$

For example, in a constituency with four seats and in which 100,000 people voted, the quota would be calculated as follows:

$$\frac{100,000}{4 + 1} + 1 = 20,001$$

This means that 20,001 votes would be required to secure election in this constituency. Any candidate achieving the quota on first preference votes is elected. Any surplus votes over the quota are redistributed proportionately to the other candidates, according to second preferences. If no candidate reaches the quota, the candidate with fewest first preferences is eliminated and all the second preference votes for that candidate are reallocated (as happens in the supplementary vote system).

Effects of the single transferable vote system

This system is the only one that provides voters with a choice between candidates of the same party. As such, it empowers the elector in a way that the party list system does not. The existence of multi-member constituencies is particularly helpful in the Northern Ireland context because of the sectarian nature of politics there.

In the 2003 elections for the Northern Ireland Assembly, 14 out of the 18 constituencies returned members from both the unionist and nationalist communities; in the remaining four constituencies, representatives of the Alliance Party were elected as well as unionists. This means that voters who feel uncomfortable about seeking the advice or help of a representative who does not share their political views have someone else within the same constituency who they can visit.

The system has firm support from the Liberal Democrats and groups such as the Electoral Reform Society. Critics argue that it is unduly complicated and lacks trans-parency, but this view is hotly denied by supporters who point to those countries where it is used with some success.

Additional member system

This system is most famously used in Germany, but a variation of it is used to elect the Scottish Parliament and the National Assembly for Wales. Voters have two votes: one for a party, and one for a candidate in a constituency. The latter are elected using the simple plurality (first-past-the-post) system. The party seats are allocated using the party list system.

This is the only system that results in two different types of representative being elected. One represents a specific body of people in a geographically defined area. The other has no such constituency to represent.

Effects of the additional member system

Elections to the Scottish Parliament and the National Assembly for Wales elect not only representatives, but also governing administrations. In Wales, Labour tried to maintain itself in office as a 'minority' administration, i.e. without having a majority of seats in the assembly. This came to grief with the resignation of the first minister, Alun Michael, in February 2000. In Scotland, Labour and the Liberal Democrats have worked well in coalition governments since the first elections in 1999. This has led to some interesting policy divergences with London over issues such as university tuition fees. Since the most recent elections to the devolved assemblies in 2003, Labour has once again tried to govern as a minority administration in Wales, but in Scotland the Labour–Liberal Democrat coalition has continued.

It could be argued that the additional member system makes minority governments more likely, but this is a complicated issue. Traditionally, Labour was able to dominate the political scene in Scotland and Wales. If devolution had happened 30 or 40 years ago, it is likely that, even using the additional member system, Labour would have governed in both Scotland and Wales with majorities. However, voting patterns have changed, and the rise of nationalist parties has meant that in Scotland Labour needs to form a coalition with another party. In Wales, where Labour has remained stronger, the party has survived for the most part as a minority administration.

Small parties often do well as a consequence of proportional electoral systems, and this can be seen in the election of members of the Scottish Socialist Party to the Scottish Parliament. Perhaps a more surprising beneficiary was the Conservative Party, which is opposed to proportional representation; in the UK Westminster elections of 1997, it won no seats in Scotland, despite polling more than 20% of the vote there, but the Conservatives did win seats in the Scottish Parliament in both the 1999 and 2003 elections.

Referendums

A referendum is a vote on a specific issue put before the electorate by the government, usually in the form of a question requiring a yes or no response. It is a contemporary example of **direct democracy**. Until relatively recently, referendums were something of a constitutional rarity in the UK, and there has only been one referendum which has affected the whole country.

Referendums in the UK

1973: Northern Ireland's membership of the UK

The people of Northern Ireland were asked if they wanted to remain a part of the UK. They voted 'yes'.

1975: UK membership of the European Economic Community (EEC)

The people of the UK were asked whether they wanted to remain part of the EEC. They voted 2:1 in favour of staying in ('yes'). To date this has been the only UK-wide referendum.

1979: devolution for Scotland and Wales
A late amendment was inserted into the Referendum Bill (The Cunningham Amendment) which required at least 40% of the electorate to vote 'yes' for devolution to come into effect. The referendums failed to meet this requirement and the subsequent fallout led to the collapse of the Labour government of James Callaghan.

1979–97: no referendums
There were no referendums during these years of Conservative government.

1997: devolution for Scotland and Wales
In Scotland voters had a two-question referendum: one was about whether to have a devolved parliament or not; the other was whether the parliament should have tax-varying powers. In Wales voters were only asked whether they wanted an assembly. The Scots voted overwhelmingly 'yes' to both questions. The Welsh narrowly approved the new assembly.

1998: devolution for Northern Ireland
The people of Northern Ireland were asked whether they agreed with the Belfast Agreement (more commonly known as the 'Good Friday Agreement'). The 'yes' vote was about 71%.

1998 onwards: elected mayors
The people of London were asked whether they wanted an elected mayor and an elected body (the Greater London Authority). They voted 'yes'. There have been a number of other city referendums on the issue of elected mayors.

Arguments for referendums
- **They enable people to decide on issues which they might not have the opportunity to consider at a general election.** Some people believe that there should have been a referendum on the Treaty of the European Union: in the 1992 general election, voters were effectively denied a say on the issue because all three major parties had given it their official support.
- **They offer another way for the public to get involved in politics.** It can be argued that voters need to be encouraged to connect with specific political issues and referendums might serve as a means of tackling voter apathy at general elections. The growth in the number and membership of pressure groups suggests that people are interested in issues, and referendums could be a means of harnessing this interest.
- **The associated campaigns can educate the public.** At the time of the 1975 UK-wide referendum on the EEC, there were massive campaigns by the 'yes' and the 'no' groups. These were accompanied by official booklets outlining the cases for and against the UK remaining in the EEC. For those voters who took the time to read all the literature available, the referendum certainly proved to be an educating

experience. It is unlikely that the public had been better informed on any issue since the Second World War.

- **They are democratic.** Referendums are an example of direct democracy. It can be argued that asking the people what they want and then acting in accordance with their wishes can only be a good thing in a democratic society.
- **There are some policy decisions that are so important that referendums ought to be used.** In recent years major constitutional decisions have tended to be referred back to the people. Clearly it was felt that the people of Scotland and Wales should be consulted before devolution in those countries went ahead. The UK's external relations with the EU fall into a similar category. There has already been one referendum on the subject, that of 1975, and the Blair government has promised two more referendums — on the EU constitution and on the single European currency. Groups such as the UK Independence Party believe that the issue is so important that there should be a referendum similar to the one held in 1975 to determine whether the UK should leave the EU.
- **They can help resolve party splits.** If a political party, either in government or opposition, is divided over a particular issue, a referendum is one way of resolving the dispute, at least in the short or medium term. In the mid-1970s, the Labour government of Harold Wilson was split down the middle on the issue of whether the country should stay in the EEC. The referendum of 1975 was as much about the government being unable to reach a decision as it was about enhancing the democratic process.

Arguments against referendums

- **The media could have undue influence on public opinion.** It has been suggested that when the referendum on the EU constitution is held, the debate will be dominated by the media. Given that the majority of the media are eurosceptic, it is unlikely that the debate will be balanced, and probable that scare stories about Europe will be prominent among the headlines. Critics claim that important decisions should not be made in such a climate.
- **Governments should do the governing.** The people elect politicians to make decisions and they are accountable for those decisions at the next general election. It could be argued that by holding referendums governments are shirking their responsibility to deal with difficult decisions.
- **Governments use them cynically.** Some people argue that governments call referendums at a time when they think they will get the decision they want. If this does not happen, they will just have another referendum at a later date, as the Danish government did over the Maastricht Treaty in 1992 and the Irish government did over the Treaty of Nice in 2001.
- **They undermine parliamentary sovereignty.** This is a very strong argument against the use of referendums. In the UK political system, Parliament is sovereign. The forum for discussion and decision should therefore be Parliament. It is argued that the increasing use of referendums will marginalise Parliament at a time when the impact of a dominant executive, the increasing influence of Brussels

and the introduction of devolved assemblies have all malignly affected the position of Parliament as the core of the UK political system.

- **People might not know enough about the issue to make an informed choice.** Although referendums are usually accompanied by extensive campaigns with mountains of literature to read, there is a fear that the public will 'switch off'. Given that television programmes about referendums need to compete with soap operas, game shows and reality TV, some critics are concerned that the turnout will be low and that those who do vote might have made up their minds on the issue without too much consideration of the arguments.

- **One side of the debate may have more resources to fund its campaign.** One of the big complaints of the 'no' campaign in the 1975 referendum on the EEC was that it was outgunned, monetarily, by the 'yes' campaign and that the resources the latter was able to deploy were a significant factor in determining the result. It can be argued that it is undemocratic that one view should predominate as a result of the financial muscle of the group supporting that view.

Political parties

What is a political party?

A political party is an organisation whose members share similar political beliefs on a number of different issues. These beliefs are usually based on an ideology (e.g. socialism). Usually, the aim of political parties is to gain political power so that they can put their policy objectives into action. They are organised to enable the communication of their messages with the electorate.

The main job of party members and activists is to gain support for their party's policies. All the main political parties have leaders who are normally elected by the general membership. The leader of a political party is often seen as the focal point of the party and as being responsible for persuading the electorate to support it in elections.

The more successful parties, such as Labour and the Conservatives, have seats in the House of Commons. The use of proportional electoral systems has led to an increase in the representation of other political parties, such as the UK Independence Party, in the European Parliament.

The functions of political parties

Making political choices coherent

Parties reduce the thousands of views that exist on scores of policies into a simpler set of choices for voters. In this way people buy into a 'basket' of policies that make sense together, although clearly there will be one or two policies in the basket which might not be as popular with some people. People choose to support a political party for a number of reasons, but finding the 'best fit' for most of the policies is a key consideration.

Encouraging participation

Parties play a major role in getting citizens to do at least the minimum of political participation and turn out to vote. They also put up candidates for election, which provides an opportunity for more active participation. Party membership offers a broad range of political activities, including canvassing, leafleting, local representation and standing for parliamentary office. Political parties help to mobilise opinion and may encourage political debate among citizens. Some political parties favour devices, such as referendums, that encourage voter input on specific policy issues (e.g. Labour and the devolution issue).

Encouraging political recruitment

In the run-up to the 1997 general election, Labour achieved a rise in its membership. Parties provide the opportunity for individuals to rise through the ranks of political institutions at local and national level. They provide the state with the future leaders of their communities and country. This is especially important when there is no tradition of independent representatives gaining any significant power in the national arena, as is the case in the UK.

Sustaining the system of government

In the UK, the government is derived from and accountable to Parliament. This is known as a parliamentary system of government. It contrasts with systems, such as that of the USA, where there is a separation of powers; in the US system, no member of the executive can be drawn from either of the houses of Congress. In the UK, it is the political party with the majority of MPs in the House of Commons that forms the government, and it is this party that maintains the government in office. If a party were to lose its Commons majority, it could no longer be assured of winning the votes necessary to get its legislation passed. Indeed, if a majority of MPs were to express no confidence in the government through a motion in the Commons, then the government would fall. Parties are crucial in this respect.

Informing the electorate

Political parties provide the electorate with information about issues and explain how they perceive a particular policy. They raise issues of public concern or, if the issues have been raised elsewhere, they add political focus to them. At election time they produce manifestos which inform the electorate of their policy positions on a range of issues. Between elections, parties consult with groups of voters in order to exchange views and promulgate ideas. This is often the case during periods when parties are in opposition. It is even true of governing parties. In an attempt to reconnect with the voters, Labour has been conducting its so-called 'big conversation', which has not only been about listening to the voters, but also about trying to explain its policies directly to the people.

Political parties and democracy

One of the important debates in this subject is the extent to which political parties promote the democratic process. The following is a brief resumé of the arguments for and against this notion.

Political parties promote the democratic process because they:
- offer the electorate a coherent choice
- educate the electorate
- encourage participation
- make sense of the electorate's choices
- facilitate accountability
- generate new ideas for changing times
- act as a training ground for political leaders of the future

However, it could be argued that **political parties do not promote the democratic process because**:
- **Party choice is limited.** Although there is a vast array of political parties in the UK, relatively few have seats in the House of Commons. As a result, voters often feel constrained to support a party that has some chance of winning. People with extreme political views are unlikely to see their chosen party getting a Commons seat.
- **Not all parties have democratic structures.** Although most parties elect their leaders, all parties select their election candidates without any reference to the wider voting public. This means that in an election voters have no choice but to accept the party's candidate or not vote for the party.
- **Parties can be run by cabals who control the party for narrow policy ends.** Margaret Thatcher was accused of this when she first became leader of the Conservative Party in the 1970s and many accuse Tony Blair of this today.
- **Collective party accountability can hurt individual representatives.** No matter how effective a constituency MP has been, if his or her party is unpopular the MP is likely to suffer a loss of votes at the next general election. If the MP is in a marginal seat, then this could lead to the loss of the seat.
- **Political parties tend to water down new ideas to fit into their own ideological framework.** They do this in order to gain wide public support for their policy programme. This often means that radical policy is avoided for the sake of political safety and it could be argued that this narrows the scope for proper political debate on key issues.

Can the UK do without political parties?

The membership of political parties has been falling while that of pressure groups has been increasing. Could political parties become extinct? The problem with envisaging life without political parties is that there is no clear indication of what would appear in their place. Pressure groups, for example, could not take the place of political parties because they serve quite distinct functions. Therefore, despite the problems with political parties and increasing public disillusionment with them, it is hard to imagine any other system being able to perform the same functions.

Adversarial and consensus politics

There is a debate as to whether the UK political system is adversarial or based on consensus. It is important that you understand these terms because they are named in the exam specification and questions will be asked about them in the unit test.

The following points suggest that **the UK political system is adversarial**, i.e. that it is confrontational and politicians refuse to come to agreement over issues:

- Traditionally, the ideologies of Labour and the Conservatives have been confrontational with little room for agreement.
- The 1980s were a graphic illustration of the degree to which politics in the UK can be adversarial — the Conservative government and the Labour opposition (especially in the early 1980s) clashed fundamentally about policy means and ends.
- Parliamentary procedures tend to be confrontational. The layout of the House of Commons, the organisation of parliamentary business and the format for questioning the executive lead to an aggressive form of politics.
- UK governments tend to be one-party; coalition governments are a rarity.
- The UK has traditionally had a two-party system. In the last 80 years, Labour and the Conservatives are the only parties to have held office on their own.
- The concepts of government and opposition mean that MPs in the House of Commons are either on one side or the other.
- Oppositions are expected to oppose. This is in order to distinguish their ideas from the policies of the government and so they act as a check on its power.

However, the above points have to be set against other factors that support the idea that **there is a degree of consensus** in the UK political system:

- Traditionally, there has been a broad agreement (or consensus) about the aims of government policy. This was especially true in the 1950s and 1960s, but it may also be true since the arrival of New Labour.
- After the Second World War there was even a broad agreement about the means to achieve the ends. The so-called postwar consensus saw very similar welfare policies from both Labour and the Conservatives.
- Some argue that in spite of the many differences that exist between the major political parties today, there are remarkable similarities between them on important issues (e.g. on the management of the economy and law and order).
- There was a marked degree of cooperation between Labour and the Liberal Democrats during the 1990s, especially over issues related to constitutional reform.
- The use of alternative electoral systems for assembly elections in Northern Ireland and Wales and for the Scottish Parliament has led to more consensus politics in those areas of the UK.

- A continued rise in support for the Liberal Democrats will accentuate this consensus trend, with further cooperation likely if there is electoral reform for Westminster elections.

One of the mistakes that students often make in examinations is to confuse consensus politics with coalition government. Clearly the two can be linked because agreement and cooperation can lead to coalition government, but often coalitions are effectively forced partnerships based on political expediency. Consensus politics should always be referred to primarily as being based on agreement about policy ends and/or policy means.

Political ideologies

The key ideologies named in the Unit 1 specification are conservatism, socialism and liberalism. This section gives brief definitions of these ideologies before summarising the key aspects of each in a table. Since AS questions are likely to be based on contemporary aspects of UK ideology and the stances of the main political parties, this information is all you need to know for Unit 1.

Conservatism

Conservatives believe in a well-ordered society based on the personal responsibility of individuals. National traditions and patriotism are important to conservatives. They are suspicious of government and therefore have traditionally supported only a limited role for the state. The creation and preservation of personal wealth and property are cornerstones of conservative thinking. Many would argue that the word ideology is not really an appropriate description of conservatism since it has tended to adapt the principles outlined above to suit the political needs of the time.

Socialism

Socialism is a broad church including a variety of views on the left of the political spectrum. At the heart of the ideology is a belief in equality, which many on the far left believe can only be brought about by the communal ownership of the means of production, distribution and exchange. The elimination of poverty and social deprivation and the eradication of the causes of inequality are all aspirations that are pursued by people who describe themselves as socialist.

Liberalism

Fundamentally, liberals believe in the primacy of individual rights. Those rights should only be restricted if they infringe on the rights of others. Personal freedoms are at the heart of liberal philosophy. Historically, some liberals preferred to stress the economic rights of the individual with regard to private property and wealth creation, which has led to some crossover between these 'classical liberals' and proponents of the New Right in the 1970s and 1980s, such as Margaret Thatcher (who was, of course, a Conservative).

Summary of key political ideologies

The table below summarises some of the key aspects of the ideologies that are included in the AS specification for this unit.

Ideology	Fundamental beliefs	Examples of policies	Variations
Conservatism	• Respect for order • Individual wealth • Hierarchy • Traditional values • Patriotism • Individual responsibility	• Privatisation • Tough crime policy • Anti-reform • Nationalistic • Smaller role for state	• Fascism • Religious right • Christian Democrat • Republicanism • Conservative • Evangelical right
Socialism	• Equality • Collectivism • Active role for state • Reformist • Internationalist • Redistribution of wealth	• Welfare • Full employment • Disapproval of private property • Rights at work • High taxation	• Communism • Social democracy • Labour • Marxism • Leninism • Democratic socialism
Liberalism	• Primacy of the individual • Freedoms • Little state intervention • Respect for rights • Reformist	• Constitutional reform • International cooperation • Human rights • Ethical policies • Environmentalism • Localism	• Most Western democracies are variations on this theme • New Right

Conservative and Labour policies

An important debate regarding political parties is the extent to which there is an overlap between the ideas and policies of Labour and the Conservatives. A key theme in politics in recent years is the similarity of the two parties, often expressed in terms of Labour having abandoned its socialist principles and traditions effectively to steal the Conservative Party's clothes.

It is an interesting debate because, like much else to do with New Labour, critics who argue that this is the case are on both the left and right of the political spectrum. Just how similar are Conservative and Labour party ideas and policies?

Similarities between Labour and the Conservatives

The economy

It can be argued that the ideas of the parties have converged in recent years, that the major ideological economic debates of the past are now over and that both parties share a broadly free-market approach to economic management. The Labour Party's abandonment of Clause IV of its constitution, which committed the party to nationalisation (i.e. the state ownership of companies), was an important symbol of this change for Labour. It could be argued that both Labour and the Conservatives are fighting to establish themselves as the party of business. As a result, Labour has been accused of deserting its traditional values, policies and supporters among the working class and the trade unions.

Social security

Both parties seek to end state benefit dependency, with Labour continuing the policy of means-testing for social security benefits, which was initiated by the Conservatives. Additionally, Labour seems keen to see people come off the unemployment register, even if this means they are going into low-paid jobs.

Law and order

On issues such as law and order and the sentencing of criminals, Labour has been accused of stealing the policies of the Conservative Party. They both share the view that there is a need for a robust response to crime and appear keen to pander to the right-wing press on issues such as asylum and immigration.

Education

The old differences on education seem to have gone, with the parties sharing views on standards and even on the issue of selection. Labour has continued with the testing regime introduced by the Conservatives and league tables remain a prominent symbol of educational standards, as does the public exposure of failing schools.

Healthcare

When it was in opposition, Labour opposed the use of public–private partnerships in the provision of state healthcare. Ironically, the only agreements to be signed for private investors to build and lease hospitals and other health facilities back to the National Health Service have been made since the 1997 general election when Labour came to office.

Differences between Labour and the Conservatives

There is an obverse to the above arguments. Labour rejects Conservative views on funding state healthcare and has been avowedly redistributionist in its taxation and spending policies. Fundamental differences of ideas also exist on the issue of Europe.

Public spending

An important difference between Labour and the Conservatives is on the issue of public spending. The Labour Party claims to have spent more money on key public services, such as health and education, than any previous government. This has caused problems for the Conservatives in recent times because they have to prove to voters that their desire to cut taxes will not come at the expense of reductions in public expenditure.

Taxation

Although Labour rejects punitive taxation to pay for investment in public services, there is no doubt that it has increased taxes. The Conservatives have dubbed these 'stealth taxes', because they are done almost out of sight of those who pay for them. Taxes on pension funds, windfall taxes and increases in national insurance contributions have all netted the exchequer extra cash to fund government spending. The Conservatives are hoping to make this an issue with which to attack the government at the next general election.

Redistribution of wealth

The Labour government has redistributed wealth from richer to poorer families. This policy would never be pursued by the Conservatives and shows links with traditional Labour policies. Although Labour politicians were reluctant to use the word 'redistribution' early on in the life of the government, many in the party now use the word proudly to draw a distinguishing line between themselves and the Conservatives.

Workers' rights

Many in the Labour Party also point to how much has been done for workers' rights since 1997. As soon as it came to power, the government indicated that it would sign the social protocol of the Maastricht Treaty. This is something that the Major government refused to do in 1992. Similarly, Labour introduced the minimum wage and has more recently reached agreement with the trade unions on the issue of new statutory holidays for all workers. On the basis of the Conservative Party's time in office between 1979 and 1997, it is inconceivable that it would have introduced such measures. Indeed, Conservatives argue that these are the very policies that will damage all that they did to create a flexible and competitive labour market in the 1980s.

Conclusion

It is clear from the above that although there is substantial evidence to suggest that the Labour Party has adopted some of the Conservative Party's ideas and policies, clear differences remain between the two parties. Claims that they are just the same are plainly untrue, since a number of policies have been pursued under Labour since 1997 which would never have been followed had the Conservatives remained in power.

Pressure groups

Pluralism

Pluralism refers to the fact that in a democracy there is a variety of viewpoints and attitudes on all issues. Pressure groups reflect this diversity of opinion. In the UK, pressure groups compete with each other to gain the attention of the government. Some compete over the same issue, but from different standpoints. For example, the pressure group Action on Smoking and Health (ASH) wants to see tougher government measures against tobacco smoking (it was partly responsible for the introduction of increasingly tough advertising controls), whereas groups representing smokers' rights, such as the Freedom Organisation for the Right to Enjoy Smoking

Tobacco (FOREST), want to see the government take a more relaxed line and not tax smokers too much.

What is a pressure group?

A pressure group is an organisation whose members have some shared interests or objectives and which seeks to influence the government. These can be formalised, well-structured bodies that have constitutions and rules. Alternatively, they can be seen in terms of movements or lobbies that might comprise a number of organisations or companies.

Classifying pressure groups

There are many ways in which pressure groups can be categorised. For the purposes of Unit 1, you need to be able to distinguish between:

- promotional and sectional groups
- insider and outsider groups

Promotional groups

These groups seek to highlight a particular issue or cause. Their members are often driven by a firm belief in the justice of an issue and seek to influence government policy on it. An example of such a group is Transport 2000, which believes in the pursuit of a more sustainable transport policy and wants to limit the growth in car use. For any issue or government policy, there is usually a cause group pursuing a particular angle on it. For example, the issue of defence is the concern of Campaign for Nuclear Disarmament (CND), which campaigns for the scrapping of the UK's nuclear weapons, but it has also recently campaigned against military intervention in Iraq.

Sectional groups

These groups usually comprise members who share a common interest. For example, they may all work in the same profession. Trade unions are the most frequently cited example of this type of pressure group. The National Union of Teachers is a sectional group because it seeks to promote the interests of its members, who are all teachers. For any group of individuals who share a common interest, there will usually be a pressure group promoting those interests. For example, the group FOREST was formed to defend the interests of tobacco smokers at a time when tobacco taxation and public disapproval of smoking were making their lives more difficult.

Problems of classification

Some pressure groups are not easy to categorise because they could be either cause or promotional groups. An example of this is the housing charity Shelter. This could be classified as a sectional group, because it seeks to improve the lives of homeless people. It also wants to raise awareness of the issue of homelessness, and in this respect the group is motivated by a cause.

Insider groups

Some pressure groups, whether sectional or promotional, have a status that gives them access to the higher reaches of the political system. They may happen to share many of the interests of the political establishment or the party in government. For example, during the Conservative Party's years in office between 1979 and 1997, the Institute of Directors proved to be an influential organisation, while the Labour government of Tony Blair has had a close relationship with figures in the Confederation of British Industry.

Some groups seem to go with the grain of the nation and of public opinion — they are almost insider groups by default. The RSPCA is a good example in this respect. The NSPCC might also be cited as an example of an insider group; it is so close to the political system that it has even been given statutory powers to handle issues concerning child protection.

Outsider groups

Other groups do not have insider status. They are on the outside and are not usually consulted on policy issues because their aims are not in line with the political order of the time. For example, in the 1980s the trade union movement was definitely outsider in status because Margaret Thatcher and her government were against any form of organised labour. The group FOREST, which defends the rights of tobacco smokers, is currently outsider in status because it does not fit in with the government's health policy and its desire to see a reduction in smoking.

The activities of some pressure groups make them outsiders. This may be because they resort to extreme measures to get their message across. Some groups in the animal liberation movement, for example, have employed terrorist-like activities. Governments normally recoil from groups that are involved in violent acts. These groups therefore have to depend on persuading public opinion in order to influence policy makers indirectly. Other groups may not employ violence, but their activities might be regarded as irresponsible by governments and this similarly makes them outsiders. For example, Greenpeace has a long history of using stunts to promote its campaigns. These attract considerable media attention, but sometimes go wrong. In one such episode the group was forced to apologise after its occupation of the Brent Spa oil platform was based on false accusations against Shell.

Changes in insider/outsider status

When examining the status of a pressure group, it is important to remember that this status may change, as the example of the trade unions makes clear. During the 1970s, trade unions enjoyed a high level of access to the governing Labour administration. Opinion polls at the time showed that many believed that the unions had more power than the government itself. This contrasts strongly with the situation in the 1980s when the unions were very much frozen out. Even with a Labour government back in power in the 1990s, the unions did not regain the degree of insider status that they had once enjoyed.

Pressure group activities

The category that a pressure group belongs to may well affect the activities that it undertakes. Insider groups, for example, might confine their activities to the quiet lobbying of those in the policy-forming community, publishing reports with the aim of getting the government to act on their findings. They might also undertake work on behalf of the government; for example, the RSPCA is authorised to conduct actions against those who inflict cruelty on animals and the NSPCC has powers in the field of child protection.

Many groups do not have this status and therefore have to resort to alternative strategies in order to achieve their aims. They often have to rely on influencing those in the policy-forming community indirectly, which they do by influencing public opinion. Activities they use might include public events, demonstrations, rallies, meetings and petitions. Public opinion is a powerful weapon and pressure groups want to demonstrate that they have public backing for their particular cause or interest.

At their most extreme, pressure groups resort to violent means in the hope that public shock might force the government's hand on an issue. Terrorism clearly falls into this category of activity. Although there is some debate as to whether groups such as the IRA are pressure groups, there is no doubt that the terrorism it undertook was intended to put pressure on the government. Naturally governments are keen to resist causes promoted in this way for fear that succumbing to this type of action might encourage other groups to act in a similar manner.

Pressure group success

The success of a pressure group depends on its status, public opinion, the media, finance and how well it is organised.

Status

The status of the group is an important factor. It can be argued that the closeness that exists between some pressure groups and the political establishment gives them an advantage and that by definition they are likely to be more successful. However, it must be stressed that having insider status does come at a cost. To maintain this status, a group needs to conduct itself in a way that does not embarrass politicians and this inevitably gives rise to questions over the true independence of such groups. Some pressure groups avoid becoming too close to politicians for this very reason — they want to maintain the integrity of their cause or interest and avoid accusations of selling out to the establishment.

Public opinion

Another important factor is the degree to which pressure groups are in line with public opinion. Groups such as the NSPCC and RSPCA stand for causes and interests that anyone would applaud publicly and consequently they find it easier to gain the support of the public, media attention and the ear of ministers.

The media

The media are vital to pressure groups. Most groups have paid press officers and the bigger groups invest heavily in ensuring that the marketing and media relations aspects of their activities are effective.

Size

The size of a pressure group can be an important factor. Governments are more likely to sit up and listen if a group has a million members, especially if it has the support of the public and media. Timing can be particularly important in this respect. Clearly, a well-supported pressure group agitating in the run-up to a general election might be hard for the competing political parties to resist. However, it is not always the case that large groups can automatically achieve success. Despite rising unemployment in the 1980s, when the trade union movement represented many millions of workers, the unions were not particularly effective pressure groups at the time.

Finance

Finance is often cited as an important factor when determining pressure group success. It could be argued that richer groups can afford to employ more and better workers, undertake more advertising and marketing, and raise public awareness for their cause more effectively than poorer groups. At the time of the 1975 referendum about the UK's continued membership of the EEC, the 'yes' campaign was a much better financed operation and this showed in the quality (and quantity) of the publicity it achieved. But money alone is no guarantee of success; for example, the Referendum Party spent over £13 million in the 1997 general election and yet failed in its main aim of promoting the idea of forcing a referendum on the issue of Europe.

Organisation

Often it is the best organised groups, which take advantage of an issue gaining sudden prominence, that are able to achieve success. There is little doubt that in the wake of the massacre of school children in the Scottish town of Dunblane in 1996, the Snowdrop Appeal group mobilised itself effectively to take advantage of the tide of anti-gun sentiment that swept the country in the months that followed. The group was able to use the pressure of the looming general election to ensure that one of the parties would take up its cause, and Labour was keen to exploit what was seen as an inadequate response by John Major's government in the immediate wake of the incident.

Pressure groups and political parties

Key differences

One important issue to consider is how to distinguish pressure groups from political parties. There are three main areas of difference:

(1) Policies

Pressure groups usually concentrate on one policy area or a narrow field of issues. For example, Greenpeace and Friends of the Earth tend to focus their attention on the environment and issues that affect it. The CND devotes itself to issues concerning nuclear weapons, but has broadened its campaigns within the confines of defence policy. By contrast, political parties offer opinions and viewpoints on a variety of issues, since voters want to know what will happen in a number of policy areas, should they be elected. At the last general election, Labour, the Conservatives and the Liberal Democrats all published manifestos that covered issues such as the economy, health, welfare, transport and education.

(2) Aims

Pressure groups, as the term indicates, aim to exert pressure on decision makers to achieve particular ends. This can be done either directly or indirectly. Examine the pressure group activities discussed earlier in this section and consider how they relate to realising certain aims and objectives. Political parties, on the other hand, seek power in order to facilitate their policies and view the pursuit of power as central to achieving their political ends.

(3) Accountability

By seeking power, political parties become accountable because they will have to answer for the actions of those who govern in their name. Pressure groups are not accountable in the same way, and a number of pressure groups are not accountable in any way, in that their leaders are not called to account for the actions of the groups. It could therefore be argued that in this key respect pressure groups are less democratic than political parties, although this general criticism can be disputed (see the section on pressure groups and democracy below).

Practical problems

Despite the distinctions outlined above, it is sometimes difficult to distinguish between pressure groups and political parties. This difficulty has been exacerbated in recent years as some political parties have emerged from single-issue pressure groups or movements (e.g. the Green Party) and other political parties have been created with one issue in mind (e.g. the UK Independence Party).

The second distinction, regarding aims and objectives, is also becoming blurred. Some pressure groups put forward candidates at election time to influence the other political parties rather than to gain power for themselves. Perhaps the best example of this was the Referendum Party which fought the 1997 general election. It called itself a party and put up candidates, but its main aim was to influence official Conservative Party candidates by threatening to stand in their constituencies if they did not back its call for a referendum on the issue of Europe. It even promised to resign from any seat it won, once its goal of a referendum had been achieved. It could be argued that the Referendum Party was a pressure group seeking to influence decision-making players in the political system.

Those groups that are intimately involved with political parties (e.g. the trade unions that are affiliated to the Labour Party) also complicate the distinction between pressure groups and political parties.

Pressure groups and democracy

One of the important debates in this topic is the extent to which pressure groups help or hinder the democratic process. The main arguments on both sides of the debate are summarised below.

How pressure groups help democracy

They are an added form of participation
It can be argued that pressure groups complement the political process by giving ordinary people an additional means of participation. This is particularly true in the period between elections, when voters may feel that they have little influence over the government, which might have 3 or 4 years left in office.

They are a measure of public opinion
Pressure groups act as an important weather vane of public opinion, of which the government and other political parties may wish to take notice. The Snowdrop Campaign certainly prompted the government to take action on gun control as well as influencing the Labour opposition to promise even tougher measures.

They are an added form of representation
Many groups are not fully represented by the formal political structures of the state. These might be minority interests or even large bodies of opinion. The workings of the UK electoral system mean that groups that have national representation in other European countries, such as the Greens, are not represented in the House of Commons. Much of the 'green' politics in the UK therefore takes place through pressure groups.

They provide expertise and advice
Some pressure groups are so well placed that when they publish reports or data the media and the government take notice. For example, groups such as the NSPCC have been commissioned by the government to conduct research on the basis that they appear more qualified to perform the task. In this sense, pressure groups can act as an important additional source of information and advice for the government. However, not all groups are in this position: insider pressure groups are more likely to be turned to for advice and information than outsider pressure groups, which will be less well trusted in government circles.

How pressure groups hinder democracy

They are unaccountable
One of the main criticisms of pressure groups is that they lack internal democracy. Many groups do not have accountable leaderships and there is a danger that groups

claiming to represent the opinions of many thousands of people are, in fact, run by a small group of individuals. Up until the 1980s this was a criticism levelled at the trade union movement, which wielded great power at a time when its internal democracy was suspect. In the 1980s industrial relations legislation was passed, which included the provision that union leaders must be elected by their members. Other pressure groups are not covered by similar legislation.

Group wealth

Some pressure groups have considerable financial resources at their disposal, for example the National Farmers' Union. As a result they are able to employ specialist staff and engage in more expensive publicity and communications. It can be argued that this means that richer groups are likely to wield greater influence within society and that this is inherently undemocratic. A counter to this argument is that wealthier groups usually have more members and should therefore be listened to more than smaller and less wealthy groups. The problem with this is that in a democracy the voice of poorer minorities should not be drowned out by that of more affluent majorities. Furthermore, not all rich groups represent large memberships, an example being the Confederation of British Industry (CBI).

Activities

Some groups behave in a way that challenges the democratic process directly. Those groups that engage in controversial, illegal or violent activities may be criticised in this respect. Some sections of the animal rights movement have resorted to actions that have put lives at risk. For example, a car bomb exploded in the 1990s killing the child of a research scientist.

Secrecy

A criticism that is often levelled at those groups with insider status is that much of their activity is done away from the glare of publicity. The feeling that these groups are exerting pressure on ministers behind closed doors, out of the view of the public, has raised concerns that there is a lack of transparency in the way that governments do business with certain groups and that policy outcomes may be decided in questionable circumstances.

Links with political parties

Some pressure groups have traditional connections with particular political parties and this could open up governments to the charge of favouritism. Many trade unions pay subscriptions to the Labour Party and, in 1997, the Conservatives warned that a future Labour government would bring the unions back to the centre of the policy-making process. Similar accusations have been levelled at the Conservatives. It can be argued, for example, that the Institute of Directors, while not formally affiliated to the Conservatives, has traditionally supported the party in elections.

Questions
&
Answers

This section of the guide provides you with four questions on Unit 1: People and Politics covering each of the main topics on the specification. They are in the style of the Edexcel unit test, which has four questions, each of which is divided into three parts.

Guidance notes after each question outline how to answer the three parts of the question and how to avoid any pitfalls. These notes are followed by A- and C-grade responses.

Examiner's comments

The answers are interspersed with examiner's comments preceded by the icon *e*. These comments identify why marks have been given and where improvements might be made, especially in the C-grade answers.

Question 1

Democracy and participation

(a) **What is a direct democracy?** (5 marks)
(b) **What are the main features of a representative democracy?** (15 marks)
(c) **To what extent has the UK become more democratic in recent years?** (30 marks)

Total: 50 marks

(a) To earn 5 marks on this question you need to give a full definition of direct democracy, including some relevant examples. A one- or two-line answer is unlikely to break into the higher mark range.

(b) This is a conceptual question which requires more than just a mechanical explanation of how a representative democracy works. It should be related to other concepts such as legitimacy and accountability.

(c) Read this question carefully and look for the key words that tell you what the examiner is looking for. The phrase 'To what extent…' indicates that you need to examine both sides of the debate as to whether the UK has become more democratic, i.e. you need to evaluate in order to gain high marks. The use of the word 'become' invites you to discuss issues which indicate that the UK has become more democratic in recent years and other issues which might point in the opposite direction. When this question has appeared on examination papers, one of the pitfalls has been for candidates to interpret it as a request for information as to whether the UK is a democracy or not, and simply to state the arguments for and against. If you do not refer to recent changes, you are unlikely to get more than 11 or 12 marks out of 30.

■ ■ ■

A-grade answer

(a) Direct democracy implies that all citizens are involved in the decision-making process, not just elected representatives. Very early examples of direct democracy were in Athens in ancient Greece. Direct democracy is not prevalent today given the difficulty of involving all citizens in the everyday running of the state. There are, however, examples of direct democracy in the modern age in the form of referendums, where citizens are consulted and are able to vote on specific issues, such as the referendums for devolution in Scotland and Wales in 1997.

e This is a good response. The candidate begins with a concise definition of direct democracy, and then gives an example of direct democracy in a historical setting and an example from recent times to show how a modern society can accommodate direct democratic principles. This balance between a theoretical knowledge of the

question

meaning of direct democracy and its modern practical manifestation in the form of referendums would earn 4 or 5 marks.

(b) Representative democracy involves electing individuals to govern on behalf of citizens. Such a system seeks to ensure that government and parliament reflect and respect the opinions of the people. In this sense, the political direction that a country takes should be in tune with the national mood. When Labour came to power in 1997 it was on the wave of a desire for change among the UK electorate. Politicians seek legitimacy from elections.

A representative assembly should reflect the make-up of its society, both in terms of opinions and of social, ethnic and gender groups. In other words, elected representatives should bear a resemblance to those people who elect them to office. It is for this reason that the '300 Group' of women MPs has been striving for better female representation in the House of Commons and why all the main political parties are striving for more parliamentary candidates from ethnic minorities.

Another important feature of representation is accountability. In such a system, the representatives must be periodically answerable for the decisions they make. The process of democratic elections facilitates accountability in a representative democracy.

There is a sense, however, that representatives are not mere delegates. Politicians are elected to govern as well as to represent and this may involve public opinion being overlooked on occasion if the political expedient is outweighed by the judgement of the representative. Many MPs used this argument to justify their decision to support the invasion of Iraq in 2003.

> This response contains a number of arguments, each of which shows a different aspect of representative democracy. The candidate explains these clearly and illustrates most of the points that are made with an example. Use relevant examples whenever possible in your answers as they will help you to gain top marks. This response would gain **13–14 marks**.

(c) It could be argued that the past decade has seen the UK become a much more democratic country. The election of the Blair government in 1997 heralded a range of constitutional changes which many argue have fitted the UK political system for the twenty-first century. Others argue that New Labour, despite its reforms, has failed to tackle the key inadequacies of the UK's democratic system. Some would go even further and suggest Labour has been authoritarian in office.

Labour has been keen to decentralise power in the UK. Soon after the 1997 general election, Labour held referendums in Scotland and Wales on the issue of devolved assemblies and devolution arrived within a couple of years. The government also appears keen to push ahead with referendums for English regional assemblies in some parts of the country.

It could be argued that these moves break with decades of tradition, in which political power has been effectively the preserve of the government in Westminster.

In addition, the fact that the government has used referendums is a move to more direct democracy in the UK.

Along with devolution came the introduction of proportional election systems for the new assemblies, making the basis for representation there more democratic than in the House of Commons. Proportional representation was also introduced for elections to the European Parliament. As a result, MEPs representing smaller political parties, such as the Greens and the UK Independence Party, have been elected.

The government has also taken the important step of abolishing the vast majority of hereditary peers in the House of Lords, whose right to sit there was based on birth. This is only the first step of reform, but modernisers believe that the hereditary peers were a symbol of undemocratic politics in the UK.

Finally, the government has introduced the Human Rights Act, which for the first time sets out clearly the rights that citizens enjoy. This means that citizens no longer need to seek redress from a court in Strasbourg because effectively the European Convention of Human Rights has been incorporated into English and Scottish law.

However, there are also arguments to suggest that the UK has undemocratic elements. The government has reneged on a promise it made before the 1997 general election to hold a referendum on electoral reform for the House of Commons. Despite other bodies having new systems, arguably the key decision-making body remains controlled by a political party with fewer than half of the votes cast in the country.

Similarly, the government has not completed the reform of the Lords and appears to be resisting an elected second chamber. Some would argue that the current arrangements are even less satisfactory than before because the government has a greater say over who sits in the Lords.

Finally, the Human Rights Act was amended almost as soon as it became law to restrict the rights of terrorist suspects. Many civil rights campaigners are calling for a written constitution, which they argue is the only way to protect the rights of the citizen fully.

On balance, despite some misgivings, the pattern of reform over recent years does point to the UK becoming more democratic.

🖉 The candidate copes well with the demands of the question. The introduction offers a broad overview before going into the specific points in detail — this is often a good tactic at the outset of a long answer as it demonstrates a grasp of the 'big picture'. The answer then deals with the specific requirements of the question: it offers a balanced analysis and tackles the issue of changes to the UK political system. It includes arguments on both sides of the debate and the conclusion reflects the weight given to each side of the argument, by coming down on one particular side. This response would gain 25–26 marks.

C-grade answer

(a) A direct democracy is when the people rule. Democracy means people power and direct democracy is when all the people in a state make all the decisions affecting them. Direct democracy is unworkable in the modern state with millions of people and that is why all Western democracies are representative democracies. Direct democracy implies that there are no elected representatives.

> *e* The candidate clearly has a basic grasp of what direct democracy is and attempts to distinguish it from representative democracy. There is even a brief statement about the unworkable nature of direct democracy in the modern age. The main problem with this response is that the candidate makes no attempt to offer any real examples of direct democracy, either from the time of ancient Greece or from the more recent use of referendums in the UK. It would gain 3 marks.

(b) A representative democracy is not like a direct democracy. Instead the people elect representatives to govern the country on their behalf. In the UK, the people elect MPs to the House of Commons and every 4 or 5 years there is a general election in which the people get to decide who is going to govern the country for the next 5 years.

Each MP is the representative of a constituency, which is a geographical area. There are over 600 of these constituencies in the UK. To elect their MP, voters put a cross next to the name of their preferred candidate on the ballot paper, and the candidate with the most votes becomes the elected representative.

MPs are accountable to their constituents because if they wish to carry on in their jobs, they have to submit themselves for re-election periodically. This means that the people can pass judgement on their representatives and that they can get rid of them if they do not feel they are up to the job.

> *e* This response contains a number of valid points that are explained quite well. However, the candidate only makes two relevant points — one in the first and one in the third paragraph. The second paragraph is merely an illustration of a point made in the first paragraph. It also displays little conceptual understanding and the focus is very much on the 'nuts and bolts' of the question. This prevents the candidate from being awarded the 11 or more marks needed to get into level 3 and to gain a grade A — the response would gain 7–8 marks.

(c) It is clear the UK has become more democratic in recent years. This is because of the policies of the Labour government under Tony Blair.

Labour held referendums in Scotland and Wales on the issue of devolution, which shows greater democracy in the country. It had been 18 years since referendums had been used in the UK.

Labour introduced devolution within a couple of years of being elected to power. The voters in Scotland supported the idea overwhelmingly, although the Welsh only approved it narrowly. Both countries now have their own assemblies, which is more democratic as it brings government closer to the people in the regions.

The government also introduced proportional election systems for the new assemblies in Scotland and Wales as well as for elections to the European Parliament. There are now MEPs for the UK Independence Party. Without the use of proportional representation, smaller parties such as these would not have been elected because of the way that the first-past-the-post electoral system benefits the bigger political parties.

The House of Lords has also been reformed. The government has abolished the hereditary peers as the first part of a reform process that could lead to an elected second chamber. The hereditary peers were regarded as an antiquated part of the UK constitution because their right to sit in the chamber was passed on from their fathers and bore no relation to their ability or worth. It can be argued that, in a modern democracy, there is no place for the hereditary principle.

It is clear that the political system has become much more democratic in recent years due to the many reforms of the Blair government.

The candidate attempts to deal with the recent changes to the UK democratic system and offers a number of points supporting the notion that the UK has become more democratic. However, no attempt is made to offer an alternative analysis, i.e. to examine the continued shortcomings of the UK political system. The answer therefore lacks the balance necessary for the candidate to evaluate effectively and so secure top marks. It would receive 15 marks.

Question 2

Elections

(a) Distinguish between a general election and a referendum. (5 marks)

**(b) Describe three proportional electoral systems currently used for elections
in the UK.** (15 marks)

**(c) What have been the effects of the use of proportional electoral systems
in the UK?** (30 marks)

Total: 50 marks

> **(a)** This question requires knowledge of two different concepts. Clearly you must write about both to earn full marks.
>
> **(b)** This question requires you to describe three proportional electoral systems in use in the UK. You should assume that there will be a maximum of 5 marks for describing each one. Therefore, even if you describe two electoral systems perfectly, you will gain a maximum of 10 marks. Most candidates will not answer perfectly and so a realistic range of marks for such a partial response is only 6–8 marks. This emphasises the importance of answering the question asked.
>
> **(c)** This part of the question relates specifically to the effects of using proportional systems in the UK. Two important points stand out. In the first place, answers should be restricted to proportional electoral systems and should not include all alternative systems. Second, examples should be for the UK and not for abroad. These points may seem obvious, but many candidates fail to spot key markers such as these and write everything they know about a topic, regardless of its relevance.

■ ■ ■

A-grade answer

(a) A general election elects MPs to a new House of Commons; it is also the means by which a new government is formed. Voters might elect their representatives for a number of reasons, including their views on a variety of issues. A referendum, however, is when voters are given the opportunity to voice their opinion on an issue by responding 'yes' or 'no' to a specific question. Referendums are a modern example of direct democracy.

> *e* This answer contains enough to gain full marks. It defines both a general election and a referendum, making the difference between the two clear. In addition, the candidate conceptualises referendums in terms of 'direct democracy'.

(b) The single transferable vote is used to elect the Northern Ireland Assembly. It uses preferential voting (where electors place the candidates in order) and has multi-member constituencies. A candidate is elected on achieving a quota of votes:

$$\frac{\text{number of votes cast}}{\text{number of seats} +1} +1$$

Votes in excess of the quota are reallocated proportionately to the other candidates using the second preferences. If no candidate achieves the quota, the one with the fewest first preferences is eliminated from the count and the second preferences for that candidate are reallocated. This continues until all the seats are allocated.

The regional party list system is used for UK elections to the European Parliament. Electors vote for a party rather than a candidate. The region is a huge multi-member constituency. The votes are added up and the percentage of votes cast for the party is translated into seats for that party. Each party has a list of candidates for each region and if, for example, there are ten seats available and Party A gets 40% of the region vote, this means that the top four names on Party A's list gain seats. Clearly this system does not involve small-constituency representation.

The additional member system is used for elections to the Scottish Parliament and Welsh Assembly. It comprises two systems in one. Voters have two votes: one uses the first-past-the-post system to elect a constituency member; the other is used to vote for a party using the list system described above. The system is designed to help parties who fail to win constituency seats receive a fair proportion of those seats awarded through the list part of the system. These are the so-called additional members. This system means that some members represent a single-member constituency, whereas the additional members do not.

This answer begins well. The candidate's description of the use of the single trans-ferable vote system in elections to the Northern Ireland Assembly does exactly what the examiner is looking for: it states the name of the system, where it operates in the UK, the main characteristics of the system and how it works. The use of the equation demonstrates a clear understanding that a quota is necessary for this particular system.

The rest of the answer follows a similar pattern in its description of the systems used for elections to the European Parliament and to the Scottish Parliament and Welsh Assembly. Note that the discussion of elections to the European Parliament demonstrates a full understanding of the relationship of the method of voting for a party to the manner in which each party's list of candidates operates.

There are just under 300 words in this excellent response which meets all the requirements of the question. This demonstrates that there is enough time both to think about and to write the necessary amount to get the top grade in the 10 minutes you have in which to answer this part of the question. The candidate would receive 14–15 marks.

(c) Clearly the introduction of these systems has led to fairer representation that more closely reflects the wishes of the voters. The anomalous situation of parties receiving hugely disproportionate numbers of votes to seats has in the main been avoided.

Proportional systems are usually fairer for minority parties; the Liberal Democrats, the Greens and UK Independence Party all benefited from the use of the regional party list system in the 1999 UK elections to the European Parliament. This was the first occasion when parties other than Labour and the Conservative Party were represented there.

Proportional electoral systems may also lead to more broad-based government. In Scotland and Wales, the use of the additional member system has resulted in coalition governments. It is difficult to maintain periods of single party governments when no single party has a majority of votes. This has meant that the Liberal Democrats have had a direct impact on policy outcomes. In Scotland, one of these is the decision not to introduce tuition fees to Scottish students. As a result, a degree of policy divergence has begun to emerge in different parts of the UK. Scotland has also seen radical socialists such as Tommy Sheridan being elected to its parliament, showing that it is not just the centre parties that benefit from proportional electoral systems.

In Northern Ireland the use of the single transferable vote has enabled a divided community to have opposed and minority viewpoints fairly represented at constituency level. In a multi-member constituency, voters are more likely to have both a nationalist and a unionist representative, which gives constituents the choice of contacting the member they feel most comfortable dealing with.

With the patchwork of electoral systems that now operate in the UK, the electoral process for electing MPs to the House of Commons is looking increasingly anachronistic. Indeed, in recent debates about an elected second chamber, the unspoken assumption was that a proportional electoral system would be deployed, which would leave the Commons system in an almost untenable position. Similarly, the policy divergences have made some wonder whether such voting systems could usher in a more cooperative form of politics in England.

Clearly, there are those who suggest that many of the electoral systems have simply managed to seize up politics in places like Scotland and Wales and that fears about the loss of strong, stable, single-party government as a consequence of proportional representation have been borne out.

🖉 The candidate identifies the effects of the particular systems used in different parts of the UK. This approach helps to ensure that all the points made are relevant and fosters the use of examples, which are important when aiming for high marks in part (c).

The Northern Ireland analysis is particularly sophisticated, not because it might seem more obscure to some candidates, but because it explains how the single transferable vote system lends itself to the nature of Northern Ireland politics.

'Higher level' points would also be awarded for the analysis and evaluation of these electoral systems on the places where they have not been introduced. The wording of this question does allow for a brief examination of the impact on politics in England.

Question 3

Political parties

(a) **What is a political party?** (5 marks)
(b) **Describe the functions of political parties.** (15 marks)
(c) **To what extent has the Labour Party abandoned its traditional ideas and policies?** (30 marks)

Total: 50 marks

(a) This question asks you to explain what a political party is. It does not ask you to describe the functions of a political party (that comes in the next part of the question).

(b) This question does not specify the number of functions you need to describe, but remember that quality is more important than quantity. It is better to make three well-explained points than four or five points which are less well explained.

(c) The key words in this question are 'to what extent'. They indicate that you must give a balanced response which considers the continuities in Labour ideas and policies as well as the changes. If you focus solely on the way that the Labour Party has abandoned its traditional ideas and policies, without examining some of the continuities in Labour policy, you will not be able to reach a level 3 mark and gain a grade A. The maximum likely to be awarded for such a response is only 18 or 19 marks, and it could be less.

■ ■ ■

A-grade answer

(a) A political party is an organisation whose members have shared or similar political beliefs on a variety of different issues, often based on an ideology such as socialism. Political parties exist to achieve political power in order to secure their policy objectives. Parties are organised to enable their messages to be communicated with the electorate. Parties have a membership and activists who undertake most of their activities. All of the main political parties have leaders who are normally elected by the general membership. The leaders of the parties are the spokespersons responsible for getting the electorate to support them in elections. The more successful parties, such as Labour and the Conservatives, have seats in the House of Commons.

e This response offers a number of the key characteristics of a political party, including structure, aims and activities, as well as some examples of political parties. In addition, the candidate makes an attempt at abstract comment, by talking about ideology. The response would score the full 5 marks.

(b) Political parties help make political choices coherent. They reduce the thousands of views on scores of policies into a simpler set of choices, enabling voters to opt for a bundle of policy preferences, especially at election time. The party manifesto offers the voter the opportunity to view all of a party's policies at once.

It can therefore be argued that parties help educate the electorate on current topics of debate. Parties provide voters with important cues about political issues. They help inform the electorate using a variety of means (such as the media).

Political parties facilitate participation. This could be no more than getting people to turn out to vote at election time, but some citizens become more involved in the political process by becoming active party members or standing for election, for example. Political parties can help citizens to feel a part of the system.

Political parties aid the process of political recruitment. They provide opportunities for individuals to rise through the ranks in politics and become the future leaders of their communities and country. Indeed, in the UK, given the system of parliamentary government, it is almost impossible to achieve any sort of national political office without being a member of a political party.

Political parties help to sustain the system of government. This is particularly important in the UK where the government is derived from and accountable to parliament. In the UK political system the party with the majority in the House of Commons literally keeps the government in office.

> This excellent answer describes five functions of political parties. Note that it is not always necessary to be this thorough to secure a grade A: three well-explained points are normally sufficient for a part (b) response, unless the question specifically asks for more. The candidate would be awarded 13–14 marks.

(c) Labour has been accused of deserting its traditional values and policies in the pursuit of political power. Figures on the left such as Tony Benn suggest that New Labour bears little, if any, resemblance to the party of which he was a prominent figure. They argue that the party has abandoned the poor in favour of wooing the middle classes and as such no longer pursues the principle of equality. By courting the business lobby and groups such as the CBI, it has also been suggested that the party leadership has turned its back on its traditional allies in the trade union movement.

The party has also been accused of stealing the clothes of the Conservative Party on issues such as law and order, and asylum and immigration matters, where the Blair government has appeared to be particularly hawkish. In this respect, some see the party, or at least its leadership, as authoritarian. The internationalist tradition within the party is also threatened by the pro-US foreign policy stance adopted by the Blair government.

Advocates of the New Labour project, however, claim that they have merely come to terms with the economic and social changes of the past 20 years. There is less attachment to 'old' preoccupations such as 'Clause IV socialism' — wealth creation and private sector partnerships are preferred instead. Traditionally, Labour placed great faith in the state's ability to deliver both economic and social progress; it talked the language of equality. More recently, the party has preferred ideas associated with opportunity and social justice.

Labour still stresses the importance of welfare services but it supports welfare reform and particularly welfare to work. It rejects punitive taxation to pay for this investment, instead relying on the so-called 'third way', combining social compassion and economic efficiency. This has once again fuelled criticism of the party from those who liken the Blair government to a watered-down version of Thatcherism.

There is another side to the debate, however, since it can be argued that Labour has not entirely abandoned its past.

Labour in power has shown a tendency towards wealth redistribution. It has redistributed wealth from richer to poorer families in its years in office, which means there are still some similarities with its traditional ideas. In addition, the party claims to have spent more money on key public services such as health and education than any previous government.

The party can also claim to have done much for workers' rights, with the signing of the social protocol of the Maastricht Treaty and the introduction of the minimum wage. More recently, it has agreed new statutory holidays for all workers with the trade unions. This suggests that many of the traditional ideas of the Labour Party can still be seen today in a number of government policies.

Indeed, the criticisms levelled at the Labour Party are in the main not correctly targeted. Many commentators believe that a change of leader, to Gordon Brown for example, would see the party steered much more firmly to Labour's past — although some cynics argue that Brown was as keen on economic and public service reform as Blair himself and that a Brown leadership would make little real difference.

Clearly, there are differences between Labour today and the Labour Party of the past, but similarities remain in some aspects of policy.

e This response covers the main demands of the question extremely well. It addresses a number of key issues and illustrates them using contemporary examples. It also attempts to tie in abstract political ideas with the key policies that have been pursued by the government over the last few years.

Perhaps most importantly, this response addresses the specific requirements of the question by offering a balanced analysis of the extent to which the Labour Party has abandoned its traditional values. It includes a discussion of the continuing similarities as well as the differences before coming to a conclusion. It would score 27–28 marks.

C-grade answer

(a) A political party is a group of people who work together in order to win power. Members share the same opinions and want to persuade other people to support them at election time. The parties publish manifestos and these contain all of the policies that the party supports. The most popular parties in the UK include Labour, the Conservatives and the Liberal Democrats.

> 🖉 This is a limited response which would be unlikely to achieve more than 2 or 3 marks out of the 5 available for this part of the question. Although the answer does include examples, these are so obvious as to be general knowledge. In addition, the scope of the response is quite narrow. The main focus of the answer is on parties fighting elections and it could be argued that this point would have been better suited to a question which asked about party activities or functions.

(b) • Political parties help provide voters with a choice at elections.
   • They educate the electorate.
   • They encourage participation at election time.
   • They act as a means of recruitment for political leaders of the future.
   • They sustain the government in political power.

> 🖉 Although this response makes the same five points as the A-grade response did, it does not explain any of them. It therefore only demonstrates knowledge and understanding and would gain just 7–8 marks.
>
> The main problem with this response arises from the use of bullet points. Bullet points tend to be a self-limiting device: their purpose is to summarise issues into short, sharp observations; they do not lend themselves to extended writing. This is not to say that bullet points should never be used. If you are running out of time in an examination it is better to include a list of bullet points than to leave a blank page, although such a response will not achieve the same marks as a piece of extended writing.

(c) It can be argued that the Labour Party under Tony Blair is completely different from the party of earlier Labour leaders. Since becoming its leader, Blair has renounced Clause IV of the party's constitution, which was a commitment to nationalisation — an important aspect of postwar Labour Party policy. Labour now wants more private enterprise, even in the NHS and education.

Labour has also distanced itself from the trade unions, which in the main fund the party and keep it afloat. This means that the old days, when union leaders were always in Downing Street discussing policy matters with the prime minister, have now gone. Some on the left think that Labour has gone too far the other way and is too close to big business.

It is claimed that Labour is no longer the party of the working class and that it prefers to look after the interests of 'middle England'. There has been much targeting of those on social security benefits and a pandering to the prejudices of some people against those who are out of work or who are asylum seekers or illegal immigrants.

Similarly, it is argued that the party's tough stance on law and order has made it much less left wing and much more like the Conservatives. This tough new stance has been criticised by many Labour traditionalists because it fails to deal with the fundamental causes of the problems that lead to lawlessness.

From the above it can therefore be seen that the Labour Party has indeed abandoned its traditional ideas and policies.

e This response makes a number of valid points. However, the answer is not as refined as that of the A-grade response. The question asked about *ideas* as well as *policies*, but this candidate has dwelt mainly on policies. These are more tangible and easier to discuss, but it is important to examine the abstract ideas on which such policies are based. If you fail to offer any conceptual analysis in answer to a question which invites you to do so, you are unlikely to achieve high marks.

The other main problem with this answer is that it is one-sided. It does not consider any continuities in Labour Party ideas and policies and so makes no attempt to offer any evaluation. This emphasises the fact that, in order to access the higher marks, you must read the question carefully and ensure that you are addressing all aspects of the question in your answer. This response would receive 15 marks.

Question 4

Pressure groups

(a) Distinguish between promotional and sectional pressure groups. (5 marks)

(b) Explain the main differences between pressure groups and political parties. (15 marks)

(c) To what extent do pressure groups help the democratic process? (30 marks)

Total: 50 marks

(a) This question requires you to distinguish between two different types of pressure group. Failure to address both aspects of the question could cost up to 4 of the 5 marks available.

(b) As with part (a), you are being asked to write about two groups: pressure groups and political parties. The key to achieving a high mark is to ensure that your answer addresses both of these fully, with relevant examples. If you address just one part, you will only be able to achieve half of the marks available.

(c) The key words in this question are 'to what extent'. They indicate that you must consider a number of arguments both for and against the notion that pressure groups help the democratic process. Your conclusion should then make a balanced judgement as to how far pressure groups help the democratic process, based on the arguments you have made in the rest of your answer. If you only look at one side of the debate, tmax you can get is 18 or 19 out of 30, and even a good one-sided response will probably only get 14 or 15 marks, which would place it in the C-grade mark band.

■ ■ ■

A-grade answer

(a) Promotional groups are those that represent a specific issue or a cause. An example of such a group is Friends of the Earth, which is concerned with the protection of the environment. Sectional groups promote or protect the interests of a specific group of people or interest. Examples of sectional groups include trade unions, such as the National Union of Teachers, and some professional associations, such as the British Medical Association, which represents the interests of doctors.

> ✍ This answer contains enough to get full marks. It examines both types of pressure group mentioned in the question. The points are well-explained and relevant examples are given.

(b) One important difference is policy range. Pressure groups usually concentrate on one policy area or on a narrow field of issues. Greenpeace, for example, focuses its attention on matters to do with the protection of the environment. The

Campaign for Nuclear Disarmament concentrates on policies concerning nuclear weapons and, more recently, on wider defence policy issues, but remains focused on a defined policy area. Political parties, by contrast, must have policies on a variety of issues because their aim is to wield political power in a number of policy areas. At a general election, political parties publish manifestos that cover issues such as the economy, welfare, transport and education.

Another difference between pressure groups and political parties relates to their aims. Pressure groups want to exert pressure on policy makers in order to achieve particular ends. Groups such as the National Farmers' Union therefore spend time lobbying decision makers both in Westminster and in Brussels. As such, pressure groups do not seek elected power. Political parties, on the other hand, do seek power in order to carry out their policy objectives. At the core of a political party's agenda is the aim of getting into office; otherwise its policies cannot be turned into reality.

Political parties are accountable. In other words, they are held answerable for the actions of those who govern in their name. Politicians have to stand for election and, if they wish to continue in a representative capacity, for re-election. The governing party has to resubmit itself to the electorate after a certain period of time. Pressure groups are not accountable in the same way. Some pressure groups are not accountable at all because their leaders are not elected by the members of the group. Consequently, it can be argued that in this respect pressure groups are less democratic than political parties.

🖉 This is a good response that has the necessary range and depth. The candidate discusses three main differences between pressure groups and political parties. These differences are well explained and are illustrated with appropriate examples. Given the relatively short time available to complete these answers, the candidate rightly focuses on the key points that need to be made, without any repetition or wandering off the point. Such precision of written communication is essential when answering this type of question. This response would be awarded 13–14 marks.

(c) There are arguments on both sides of the debate about pressure groups and democracy. It could be argued that pressure groups help democracy because they are an added form of participation. This is particularly true in the period between elections. Pressure groups have been active since the last general election in trying to get their message across. An example of this would be the many groups who came together under the 'Stop the War' banner in the run-up to the invasion of Iraq in 2003.

Pressure groups are a measure of public opinion. This means that, on a range of issues, political parties can gauge the views of the electorate, and it can be argued that governments can be responsive to the views of the people. In the 1990s, following the Dunblane killings, the Snowdrop Campaign prompted the government to take action on gun control.

Pressure groups can be seen as an added form of representation. The majority of groups are not represented in parliament. These may be small groups but some large bodies of opinion might also go unrepresented in the House of Commons. The first-past-the-post electoral system means that some groups' opinions are not represented in the Commons even though they do receive national representation in other European countries, such as the Greens in Germany, for example. Most 'green' politics in the UK are therefore voiced through pressure groups such as Greenpeace and Friends of the Earth (although the Green Party is enjoying more popularity in the UK).

Finally, pressure groups provide expertise and advice to elected politicians. When some pressure groups publish reports or data, the media and the government take notice. Groups such as the NSPCC have been commissioned by governments to conduct research on the basis that they appear more qualified to perform the task.

Pressure groups may hinder democracy, however. In the first instance, they are unaccountable. One of the main criticisms of pressure groups is that they lack internal democracy. Many groups do not have accountable leaderships and groups that claim to represent the opinions of many thousands of people are in fact run by a small group of individuals (the trade unions up until the 1980s, for example).

Some pressure groups are very wealthy. Richer groups are likely to wield greater influence and this is undemocratic. It can be argued that the voices of poorer groups should not be drowned out by those of more affluent organisations.

Some groups behave in a way that directly challenges the democratic process. Those groups that engage in controversial, illegal or violent activities may be criticised in this respect. Some sections of the animal rights movement have resorted to actions that have put lives at risk. Some would argue that the activities of groups such as Greenpeace are also undemocratic (as in the case of the Brent Spa oil platform in the 1990s).

This is a full and balanced response which addresses the question directly; it would achieve 25–26 marks. There are no rules about how many points you should make overall or the number of points you should include on each side (unless the question specifies this); you could get a grade A without necessarily making all of the above points, but clearly the more points you make the greater the breadth of knowledge and understanding you will demonstrate to the examiner, as long as you explain each point well. Similarly, you should not be too concerned if you make more points on one side of the argument than the other. It may well be that your response contains four points in favour of a particular proposition and only two against. The key point is that you have demonstrated skills of evaluation (AO2) by offering arguments on both sides of a particular debate.

C-grade answer

(a) A promotional group looks to fight on issues such as health. Sectional groups are different because they want to fight for groups of individuals who have something in common, such as a job.

> *e* Although this answer refers to both of the types of pressure group required by the question, it would not achieve full marks because the explanation lacks precision and no real examples are given. It would be given 3 marks.

(b) There are two main differences between a pressure group and a political party. Parties want to get elected to power and therefore put up candidates in elections. Pressure groups, on the other hand, do not put up candidates in elections because they do not seek elected office. Pressure groups want to influence those in power, the politicians, by a variety of means. Another difference between pressure groups and political parties is the fact that pressure groups usually only have one aim and they confine themselves to that area of policy, such as Greenpeace and the environment. Political parties have ideas and plans on a wider range of issues such as defence, health and education as well as the environment.

> *e* This response is mainly held back to a grade C because of its limited range. It contains only two substantive points, whereas the A-grade answer contained three. However, if the candidate had explained these two points in more detail, and offered more examples to back them up, this response might have been worth more than a grade C. It is important to remember that the quality of your work is often as important as the quantity. This response would receive 7–8 marks.

(c) Pressure groups can help democracy because they allow for extra participation. They therefore help people get more involved in politics. When people go on demonstrations or marches, such as against the Iraq war, they are getting involved in the political process in a way they might not otherwise. Participation is seen as a good sign that democracy is working.

Pressure groups may also provide expert advice to the government. This can be in the form of data or reports that are put together and then published and sent to ministers. This means that they are providing information from the front line, as it were, and those in power might find it useful when making future policy decisions. This work could also save the government time and money in setting up its own reports or commissioning its own surveys.

Pressure groups can be seen as an additional type of representation. The big political parties often do not reflect the opinions of some individuals, especially those with strong opinions on certain issues. By definition, the parties need to have opinions on a wide range of issues and cannot devote too much time to individual ones. These opinions do not get aired in parliament. Pressure groups can be seen as a way of giving these issues a voice in the country.

question

Pressure groups hinder democracy because they are unaccountable. Many groups do not elect their leaders and are therefore not answerable to the people who pay their subscription fees to the pressure group itself. This means that ordinary members have no way of getting rid of their leaders if they become unpopular or take decisions for which there may be disapproval.

Some pressure groups have a lot of money. Such groups may have more influence over the political process and this could hinder democracy. In a democracy, the amount of money a group has should not determine how much power and influence it has.

e This response is balanced, but it makes fewer points overall than the A-grade response and its explanations are not as insightful. It does not give any examples of the activities of particular pressure groups. One important point that is omitted, and which should have been included, is the illegal activity referred to in the A-grade response. This response would achieve **17** marks.